Praise for
Gatherer's Alphabet

What I love about Susan Kelly-DeWitt's poems are the colors, how they "hold / themselves out / to be touched." Her mother is described as having "storm-colored hair." Silence is a "white bulb." The past is a minefield of blue flowers. This bringing together of nature and mind, the mundane and the transcendent, is the result of the poet's unrestrained sympathy for all living things. Kelly-DeWitt's companions in this vision-quest are O'Keeffe and Van Gogh, artists who paint not the appearance of field and cloud, but the primal energy beneath the surface. The act of seeing is the true subject here. We are fortunate to have Kelly-DeWitt to guide us through this journey.

—Michael Simms, editor of Vox Populi, author of *Nightjar*

Coming from a world "sheltered by cold leaves of starlight," Susan Kelly-DeWitt's powerful new work serves as a garden for ghosts, windows, and angels capable of making ordinary events extraordinary. A sharp sense of loss is integral to *Gatherer's Alphabet*, which is steeped in the particulars of memory, the pebbles, the dark pits. Here is an "impossible country of imagination" that must be visited over and over.

—Maya Khosla, Poet Laureate Emerita of Sonoma County, author of *All the Fires of Wind and Light*

Gatherer's Alphabet

Poems

Thank you!

Susan Kelly-DeWitt

Susan Kelly-DeWitt
11/26/22

Gunpowder Press • Santa Barbara
2022

Published by Gunpowder Press
David Starkey, Editor
PO Box 60035
Santa Barbara, CA 93160-0035

Cover image: Detail from *Maple Leaves* by Shibata Zeshin.
Open Access image courtesy The Metropolitan Museum of Art.

ISBN-13: 978-1-957062-00-6

www.gunpowderpress.com

What future race in the ruins
will trace out our shape from the bent
template of the soul...?

—Dennis Schmitz, "Making Chicago"

"There will be another dictionary, traced out of ash,
that aligns the day with the night."

—Judy Halebsky, "Addendum: Fifth Moon"

Contents

I.

II.

III.

IV.

I.

Calling The Horses

You whistle
and they turn their heads—

A roan mare pushes up slowly
from the dusky pasture grasses;
a palomino and a chestnut bay
follow in sequence behind her—
they move toward us
without conviction. The mare's
belly slumps with the weight
of her unborn foal, as we call to them
across barbed wire.

(In our minds we beg
for the victory of their close looks,
but they stop, refuse to look longer,
turn away the grazing darkness
of their eyes, fall back to each other.)

Wild oats silver the fields, bluebottles
leap up along the roadside
in four fringed colors. I stoop to gather
a few wild panicles—
the crushed juice of the broken
stems perfumes my thumbs.

It feels like beauty,
the way the colors hold
themselves out
to be touched.

My Mother at Evening

Look how the rays of late
sunlight break around her,
tinting her storm-

colored hair; the way tawny
specks of sunset silt
the sleeves of her sky

blue blouse and pink motes
halo her thin silhouette,
as she stoops

to gather early stardrifts, nectarine
daylilies. Look
how that frail

curvature, that tissue-fine
remnant of bone and hope
still struggles to light inside

her body, as she bends
to tug a weed from between
pale roots or trowel

clumps of dirt from a berm,
as if to unbury
something secret,

a white bulb
of silence.

Hummingbird Sutra

Every live bird
is a thrumming under the ribs—

the song sparrow, *melospiza*
melodia, wearing clear feathers of wind;

even tyrant crows, that hunger and glint
                    lift like beauty
in my throat

but

when a hummingbird hangs
                    like a small wheel

                    of fire

above a bleeding
heart's hooded inner
life

when it pierces
a sunflower's honeycomb

                    eye

                    to suck the rough
                    sweetness

or dips to sting

a ragged fringecup
with its bliss

I want to shake myself
loose,

fledge

iridescent feathers
of human song.

Lily Sutra

The tufted Swamp
Onion from high wet
bogs; Soap Plant
used to stupefy fish,
the crushed roots
tossed in raw, seeding
a creek with paralysis;

the Death Camas, whose
tender leaves reek
poison.

All spring the true ones
tumble up from clumsy
graves, meek as handmaidens
at first, then fisting
forth tight buds.

Some years, rich or poor,
whether I've lived
generously or not,
they float like stars
in my garden: Empress,
Tiger, Leopard, Turk
and the ones called
Enchantment.

Critic

The mixture of blues in the delphiniums
colors in the spaces of the mind's

arboretum on this windy day in autumn—
and the cedar waxwing, who bows to tip

his crest to me from a shady fence post
outside my studio window—who studies me

with his cat-burglar face—flies off again,
uninterested in the hothouse poem

I am trying to construct, this cramped
conservatory of words where sounds are all

steamed up, and I am cross-pollinating
syllables, hybridizing memory and myth.

Two Butterflies and a Spider

This afternoon I saw two butterfly
lovers in the bohemian vine—western
tiger swallowtails broken

into parts by the squares of the study
window; when they paused
in the middle of one

pane, they became whole
again, perfect black lace
and lemon silk fans.

And I saw but did not disturb
the orb-weaver's delicate web—
My poet says a poet should be

like the gray anonymous
spider, whose busy feet
map the hidden...

(Or, I think, like ogre spider
who carries her web on her back
and slings it to trap

whatever she needs
to live.)

After My Mother's Death: Forget-Me-Nots

Resilient,
they grow under
and between things,

in sunny fields, in damp
meadows and marshes, along boggy
streams—"bright-eyed floweret

"of the brook,
Hope's gentle gem"
Coleridge called them—

each wheel with its little sun-spokes,
its toothless gear
of pollen; carrying

on where they may,
as if delighting
in themselves; a scent

like wisteria
blossoms, antithesis
to sorrow, while

the memory of the mother self-
sows, while the past
becomes a border

of rampant blue, a mine-
field of small but true
blue flowers.

Sewing Box

Half-hidden, her thimble,
little dimpled well.
What residue
of her salt
does it contain?

(The chary bird in me
loves to sip from it.)
Measuring tape, scissors...
Enough equipment here
for the tedious Fates.

Yes, here is her favorite
pincushion, the sharps
and darners stuck in it
like small, heroic
swords.

Cloth Doll with Found Feathers

She's tacked,
hemmed, mended
and since, like us, she hides
her past, her back is
sutured, the twisted
knots looped tight
as koans or sutras.

—A totem for midlife?

Gravity pitches her
splayed limbs akimbo;
her cloth so thinned
we see clear through
to the eggshell ghost
of stuffing underneath.

Her smile is mystical:
realistic but tidy.
Her winter berries
are wired on, like her hoop
of crow and pigeon
feathers, palm frond skirt.

(Before birth, in an alternate
life, her body was
scraps; she polished cloudy

bureaus, buffed them up,
then retired, anonymous
and calm.)

Softness extrudes
but holds her
steady. Pliability
erects her.

after a sculpture by Lisa Culjis

Angel with Cabbage Leaf Wings

> *"The image became more human and turned into an angel."*
> —Jorjana Holden

She squats in the yard
beside the old remedies—
feverfew, spleenwort, teasel

and the molds: stunning
death cups, mossy
penicilliums.

Salts rise through
her bronze heft, tensile
limbs, and rush

into her blooded,
dependable breasts.
Imagine

varicose wings,
waxy, pink, ash-
green leaves, rooted

in the gardens of flesh,
not myth—so unlike
those first, terrifying

angels, alloy of wrath
and fire, sent to guard
the perfect world.

after a sculpture by Jorjana Holden

Snow Queen

At the shelter Rhonda paints
thick yellow tulips with broad green stems

on newsprint with tempera then
draws black bars over every blossom

"to lock the bad man in jail."

"I am the bride of Christ," she insists.
Her eyes are onyx beads in a face white as Eucharist.

She's like a bird or a broken mirror, reflecting
bright feathers of a former self.

(The eyes retreat to some bedroom in her skull.
The past breathes there, under blankets on a cot.)

She's listening to an inner radio, a crystal set
no one sees, except sweet Jesus. There's static today.

Still, her husband might be hiding
in that babble. She's been searching for him

everywhere—says he beat her up for being
a virgin on their wedding night—

Don't you even know how to fuck?

—says he left her when their boy died
of leukemia. Outside, the beautiful dread

snow begins

to fall again

"Look!" Rhonda shouts—"It's the Snow Queen!
The Snow Queen is coming!"

in slow motion at first, then faster
                                        and faster, until it stings
the eyes like
wedding rice.

Static

She sits cooling in the shadows, hips immersed, knees
        disappearing in fluid arcs, dappled curvatures

like some heavy shorebird rinsed in light, beside plumes
        of willow. She would paint herself in as part river-

bird if she could, stroke her arms iridescent, blend her
        tearstained face to oxide wings ruffled over ocher

cliffs on the opposite shore; her fleshy thumb is shaded in next
        to milk-veined quartz. Here ancient mudflows cemented

oxbloods and ivories, skull bones of horses, a white scum
        of volcanic tuff. The thought of suicide muscles the picture

once—twice—three times. She blots out all the radio
        voices that could drive her to it—"booze

devils," her mother would have called them.
        The woven crucifix on her neck

is wet with sweat. The clouds
        oppress her like low flying angels.

Brother Mockingbird

Charismatic Movement, 1972

Mockingbird, you speak in tongues as I once did
when I was young

and traveled the circuits of the faithful strange.
Was it your complicated song

that rose and multiplied from the basement of Saint
Francis Church on L Street, as your cousin

the Holy Spirit descended upon the crowd? I suppose
somewhere in the attics of Time

the ghosts are still gathered there, arms uplifted,
conducting Spirit with electrified

tongues. (I must exist there also, shadow-self,
peel of atoms, the tempest in my mouth

a full blast audio, taste buds prickling
with sanctified noise; impossible to understand

without some impromptu autodidact
of glossolalia to step forth and translate.)

Mockingbird, good brother! You are a workhorse
of a workingbird this morning!

hauling your hearty chapel of repertoire,
your steady hopeful stream of fluctuating trill—

apostle of gloss, tail feathers pumping, holy
lowercase unroller of song.

Van Gogh, *Landscape at Twilight*

A feverflower and toadflax shine

laid on in strokes like agitated flocks
of birds fanning out behind the layers of visible

twilight. Wheat and marigold colors. An ochre
road bisects the fields and ends where sight does

in two pinched-off nubs, like the short dark strings Atropos
will soon cut off. (The same road painted by another

could brighten again at sunrise, might continue on
through the tangled fig-violet thicket he has wedged

at the horizon, beyond the iris roof of the chateau

————————

between pear trees.) Someone leans through a window,

gone long ago to ruin, in the musk of evening's damp
grain and floral scents. A single quick stroke of ivory

black conceals her figure in a sunless brick
of shadow. We see—or imagine we do—

how one bare arm stretches deliciously into the oncoming
night, into the racket of blue flies, while the sun turns

————————

everything to fire again, then dies.

(That blue roof still holds steady against the torrent
of sky.)

Morro Bay Sketch

I saw the comb jellies gleaming, beached
ink and crystal, in the sea wind's
cold fire, and

the egrets waiting, wading,
waiting; their sickle necks muscling
under the quartz

feathers, the beaks harpooning,
working the weed-wrack
and foam-lip—

juggling up a flash, a hopeless
flip and urgent splash
of writhing

through the sand-grit
and surf-crack. Was there
some calligrapher hiding

in the cloudshift that wrestled
and boiled in over them—
some itchy finger

or twitchy nib that sketched them in,
that outlined them all over
with restless mercury?

How the River Sleeps

The crows must recite
                    Bloodnight, Bloodnight...

          Then the hook-
jawed woman who unreels
every barbed and dazzling thing, every net
of torn sparkle and trouble, every raveled
                    molecule of
                              rainbow and
                                        knife—

the shifty one who spins shafts of black
light and drownings, moth
mullein and deadly nightshade
                    atoms, seep
                              spring monkey
                                        flowers and stinging
                                        nettle—

tiptoes from her lonely cave;
kneels among cattails and scouring
                    rush; whispers:
                              shhhhh,
                                        shhhhh,
                                                  shhhhh...

She hums and wheedles and strums
all the little strings
                    of cold persuasion.

I Ordered a Dragonfly

I ordered a dragonfly to take flight—
    I launched a cliff swallow
        like a paper airplane

      out over the river
    and I commanded them to find
the blue boat

that carried my father
    away one November,
        the boat that bore

      my mother
    with her paralyzed left side
to the mouth of the sea.

The dragonfly refused,
    the cliff swallow circled back
        to his perch in a willow,

      as if they both knew
    the boat was made of ghost-wood, sealed
with ghost-wax.

The Kiss

My mother asks why
the dogwood leaves have turned
brown, sour, as if some hint
of morbidity had worked its way
upward from the soil, leaving
the berries untouched.

I won't tell her I saw my father
under the dogwood's blight,
sheltered by cold leaves
of starlight—that he touched
his fingers to his blood-bright
lips, and blew me a kiss.

Wedding Guest

I forgot to ask her
what kind of feather
she wore in the velvet cloche
pinned so tightly to the close
short curls of dark hair that bore
a semblance to those marble
spirals carved on the august
heads of Roman generals.

In the restroom she said
"My husband wants to divorce me"
—because she was "tipsy,
talking too much," because,
she said he said,

she hugged the bride and delivered
an unscheduled toast, because
she spilled a few drops of red wine
on her sleeve and wore
an iridescent retro
suit that shone in the sun
like tarnished gold;

because she gave a speech
that turned heads, that hinted
at cancer; a speech that had baldness,
and wigs, and chemo in it,

and a love poem
by Burns.

The Thorne Miniatures: English Bedchamber Jacobean or Stuart Period, 1603-1688

The ornate Jacobean cupboard doors (carved
with flowers or suns) hide any linen or sachet
scents, like shut trumpet blossoms at night.

The bed reflects the influence of exile (to scale)—
Charles II and his court in France, where visitors
called on nobility abed in late, fashionable walnut.

A needlepoint falcon swoops on a high-back chair:
Turning and turning in the widening gyre...so anyone sitting
is prey. The canopied bed is draped with rich mint

damask, inviting the wealthiest ghosts (modeled
on the Spangled Bedroom at Knowle). There's a silver
bowl with fruits the size of a tiny porcelain doll's

eyeballs. Greenery in needlepoint sprouts
on the paneled walls while the dressing table poses
one glass sequin, iris of mirror, reflecting the small

but true. Here even God's thoughts must shrink
to kneel on the itsy bitsy prie-dieu.

Angel Behind Bars

Paris, 2006

It was hard to tell if they were raising or lowering it
into or out of the Parisian light. Angel that could be

measured in years or tons—weather-worn, pitted, gray,
like all the old ideas of heaven.

(If a crane had played God, it had vanished for the day.)
There was a turquoise strap chained to its throat,

as though a piece of sky had been torn into scraps
to tether it steady. If faith is a dark cellar,

the angel's feet were just a few steps away.
And the bars? Okay,

they were only the guardrails above the cellar stairs—
still, the eyeless eyes held something

prisoner there.

The Reliquary of St. Therese of Lisieux Comes to the Cathedral of the Blessed Sacrament

Cameras flash: */*/*/
Briefly

the Little Flower lived
with a holy ardor.

I will let fall from heaven a shower
of roses, she wrote, tubercular. *Everything is*
grace. An overhead speaker signals:

Five minutes left
before the bones disappear,
whisked away in an Explorer

to a convent in the hills. Panic
surges—
all of us gathered here to see, to touch
the plexiglass dome
that houses the bones
in the gold-trimmed
box of
jacaranda wood.

Everyone shoves,
cutthroat: hope's mob.

—Sacramento CA, January, 2000

Maybe I Have No Ideas

Eating a turkey sub from the school cafeteria
I suddenly think of the blonde woman
whose marriage is falling apart and the dark
circles under her eyes, as if two moons
had lost their light there; I think of how
she so unevenly layered the pickles and tomato
with the pink turkey flesh and the odd way
she has of wearing what she calls a "wife-beater"
T-shirt, even in winter. Her fingers have left
their slender depression in the bun, so in
this tangential way we touch. And then
it strikes me that maybe I have no ideas at all
of my own, only other people's lives where
they've left their imprint on my husk.

II.

Callas

The calla's made for you to paint...
—Anita Pollitzer to Georgia O'Keeffe

She's out in a dusty field
painting the white funnels
stubbed with nubs of butter

color, her ivory shirtsleeves
spattered in oils, scrolled
up over thick, useful wrists.

No matter if the field's in her
mind: There's a burning, a wind
wild as loneliness; an open space

between two faraway ridges.
The callas unfold slowly,
reluctantly. She grows stubbornly

toward each flower, like an eye
toward its only light.

Jeffers at the Edward Weston Show

Crocker Museum, Sacramento, 2004

There's a confluence
among things—

the shoulders of a pepper
the buttocks

of a pear, cruciferous
vegetables

and riverine channels
of shadow

in a dune's dry tributaries;
the flare

of light on an upper lip's
down,

the trunk of a cypress, the surf
off Point Lobos,

the riffles of a dead
pelican's feathers

and the famous hawk profile of
the California poet.

Maggie's Garden

Belief in the ordinary is planted
in scarlet hedgerows along a south-facing fence.
Everyone who comes to admire the garden takes away
a twig, a leaf, a branch. And when the wind comes
up in the evening (as it does) from the southwest

milky translucent pods waft down like tissue
paper moons, like ideas encased in isinglass,
glossy flecks of potentiality cushioned inside
each one; like an artist's eye, which absorbs it all
spongily, which marks a position and coordinate

for each and every rootlet, each filament of possibility;
for each least flea of conceivability, each passion flower
of limitless desire trellised against doubt (twined
around the fruitless suspicion that the common
hairs on the head of a daylily pistol might be counted

only matter and therefore become immaterial
to some possible manifestation of the truly divine
in a hooded junco asleep in the chartreuse tupelo)
and a faith in the cerise poppy's blue-black corolla as nothing less
than the peaceful coexistence of nectar and delight—

the seed of a thought which tonight Maggie will render
visible as Van Gogh's *Starry Night*, as she swirls
her sable brush in incarnadine inks, and bows to the garden,
and paints in the hollyhocks flaming, and the cosmos flaring
wildly in the northwest corner of her verdant memory.

—for Maggie Jimenez

Watercolor

In another life he spoke Japanese, lived
in Japan, captained a ship, moved to Belize,

worked in a steel mill, boxed for two years,
went back to school, got his degree, taught

English, learned Spanish and French, fished
Alaska, settled in Portland. He's retired now, bent

over a watercolor block in art class—sketching
a horse with a number two (crest and withers,

croup and loin, forelock and throatlatch)—working
from an old photograph he snapped at fifty-three:

A stallion in a wheat field. He draws it on open
sea, chooses phthalo and cobalt for the tableau

of waves, with a touch of arctic white.
He wants a horse that can walk on water.

a New Testament horse.

Two Geishas on an Anonymous Print, 1923

One is reading by lantern light, a letter from across the sea. The other is thinking how any Mt. Fuji can rise up inside a snow-capped mind. (They look fused yet independent, kimonos cut from separate cloth.) *I see... they're on deck aboard a ship. The ocean is their promenade; whitecaps lick at their sleeves, a reminder that all is salt and froth.* Underneath their hearts could be stern, not geishas at all but spiritual Carmelites. The waves break into fifty little claws.

Magpiety

Their fervor today is worms.

According to the gospel of magpie,
survival is a tasty creature.

Listen!

They're preaching a peckety-peck-peck
sermon on self-sufficiency.

They squawk their *glossolalia*
dressed in jazzy cassocks.

They proselytize rapture then ascend
from a wobble of heavenly

bamboo.

Sonnet

This morning we walked the neighborhood—cool breeze, partly cloudy sky above the canopy of leaves. A magpie invited us to join him for a while (his tuxedo lacked a bowtie). He could have been a waiter or a butcher gussied up to wed (wait: let me harness an errant line: blood is the garnet sash on the flesh of a soldier. Graveyard rhetoric. A line for a poet-general. Major segue: dogwood's blood, out of the blue—) Canopy, panoply of leaves... Later: Sleep. We walked a neighborhood of clouds—smoke was rising from a lake, its cold patina. Then the lake was the smoke. An old woman handed me a paper fortune—"The only certainty is that nothing is certain" (proverb posing as fortune). After that God dropped in as a dragonfly in garnet drag, and I begged It for mercy. The fortune became a harness. God could have been a waiter or a butcher or a soldier, but arrived as a dragonfly in that smoky emirate. I woke and consulted Jung. *Anyone who takes the sure road is as good as dead.* Those words then in my partly cloudy head.

The Sea, Cape Split, 1939

After John Marin

The huge rocks,
like coals to fire
the furnace that tricks
sailors, are tame

beside it.
And do you think
that's the sky you see—
that innocent ribbon

of blueberry cream
far out where gulls
escape like savage
angels into invisibility?

Here two terrors
are joined by a white
seam, a dinosaur spine
of the sea's rage.

A cloud of rabid
spume breaks over
a distant shoal
as if to swallow it.

The Presidio

San Francisco, 1947

He has just lost thirty-six holes of golf.
He stands, leaning over his clubs, his hands
resting lightly on the gloved woods.
There is a hardness in his grain.

(He has been stateside only six months
four years since the terrible Buna Campaign
he will not speak of, though once I heard
"cannibalism" when he was drunk.)

Some nights he screams in his sleep, dreaming
jungle. Even before he enlisted, a battlefield
existed inside his wild and terrified heart.
His first wife left him, too full of his dark

moods. "Strong as a bull," his brothers said.
"Once he pulled a car, chained to his chest,
three city blocks, like the Strongman in a circus."
(His muscled body is hidden under his baggy clothes.)

He is about to put his golf bag away, into the trunk
of his '43 Chevy. He should drive home now,
to his wife and newborn daughter but he will not.
Instead, he will walk a hundred paces to the Officer's

Club bar. There he will start with one drink, then two—
soon he will buy drinks for all his buddies. He will play
blackjack and stud poker most of the night, until he wins
or loses everything. Long after the moon rises

over the battlements of the old Spanish garrison,
over the windswept pines, the fragrant eucalyptus, the cannons
still pointed out to sea, he will stumble into the night.
Caught by passing headlights, the small

white woven deer on his sweater will seem to leap
across his chest wall. His heart is already wounded.
For twenty years he will carry its torn carcass
inside him. —Twenty years!—The pulse

of a heartbeat in time—captured here, in this photograph, this single cell sliced from time: Heartskin,
genetic memory. From his future, I foresee my past:
Lit by moonlight, he will appear, then vanish

like a jinn into his bottle.

Love's Animal, 1958

This is the night Uncle
will be carried away by his love affair
with drink. The Seven Sisters police the sky
until the paddy wagon arrives. (He doesn't realize
I've been smuggled out a bedroom
window, to summon the law

from a neighbor's phone; he rages on
inside the three-family house.) His face wears
liquor's dull polish when the cops ring the bell;
his tattooed knuckles rap L-O-V-E-U
against the bars

as they lock him in. He's love's animal
tonight. His wounded cat-cry whines at us
when the wagon skids from the curb.
It sounds like refrain,
like singing.

Toward the Music

Even in the womb she played,
tapping weightless iambs against
her mother's insides—such a sorrowful
tune, like those sad Irish lullabies;

as if she understood the language
of salt, the rhythmic constrictions
of the woman's body. And when the man
locked the woman outside

in her nightgown, so that silk chilled
the body's thin cloth, the girl rocked
under the web of polished stitches,
writing the only poem she knew,

using the pressure of her tiny knees.
And when the man split the woman's lip
so that it hung like the flap of a gutted
fish, the woman did not cry out but

the girl's fist spasmed in the amplified panic
of her mother's heart. And in the womb
she heard—yes!—her grandfather fiddling,
his angular arms coaxing the resonant dark.

Words

Some seed themselves in the moist heart
like nasturtiums. Some die back, refuse
to grow, so the old man in the rocking chair
hangs his head, swallows hard, erases
today—doesn't want to think about tomorrow.

Some arrive like sleepwalkers, alone
in their solitary rambling, who will not remember
the drawers they open, the windows,
the secrets, the doors.

Others float on a wave of ocean or sunlight,
with salt on their tongues. Flushed and naked
they build sandcastles in the air then turn away
from each other, preferring silence
to spilling their dreams or singing a song
into the cold winter nights of a poem.

Tomorrow, another sunrise—
the morning will be full of erasures,
and scribbles on a page.

after Lola Haskins

To My Mother on Her Seventy-Sixth Birthday

August 12, 1995

the hard green fingers
of the trumpet vine beckon
evening approaches

the fountain at dusk
swallows its own music—sad
notes in dying light

a night wind walks by
whoosh—dark eyes, an old gray head
enter the forest

1.

there was a secret
book in your heart, it was a
book of poetry

written by you if
you'd had a different life
with a grass linen

cover and embossed
letters like bamboo, it was
autographed by you

out of the mother
out of the hull of the ship-
wrecked being I come

2.

Who made the world? I
asked you once years before you
could hear, as the dust

of stars gathered me
from the void's farthest edges
a drift of unborn

far out on the string
of your being I floated
I waved like a pale

handkerchief, *hello…*
when the sea wind pounded waves
on Kona's lava

ledges, when it churned
greenish white along the black
sand beaches where you

collected sea snails
and played your childhood games, I
felt how you carried

me in your pockets
like an unwritten letter
I circled above

you like a hundred
wild white birds, calling, calling
white feathers of me

3.

falling around you
softly as a breath of snow
you looked up beyond

and through me as if
straining for a glimpse though I
was less than a mist

almost as if you
heard me after all, my unborn voices which were

not yet one voice, one
sad song woven from yours, voice
spun from silence—all

the years you sat still
at your school desk, not speaking
unless spoken to

I was braided like
ribbon into the tamed gloss
of your onyx hair

whenever you dipped
your fountain pen in peacock
blue ink, droplets of

my uncreated
being oozed from the pen—I
was almost a word

4.

out of the mother,
out of the hull of the ship-
wrecked being I come

with ash in my hair
with ash in my mouth but still
singing hymns, praises

oh sky oh sea oh
clear blue air, singing hymns and
praises to silent

mothers whose bones burn
clean, whose flesh turns into air
whose words were never

spoken, whose poems
were never known never sung
oh there are thousands

of such women, such
lovely women with poems
locked tight in their hearts

words chained to their lips
struggled words, strangled tales, joys
even joys untold

5.

the hard green fingers
of the trumpet vine beckon
evening approaches

6.

your quiet mother
her composed sadness in its
ivory dress, lace

of bones, and her own
mother, immigrant soul—who
went blind from stitching

other people's clothes
the one who came round Cape Horn
on the *High Flyer*

a four-month journey
who gave birth in steerage, fed
the baby crumbs (told

how even the crew
learned to starve), who blessed the ground
when she walked on it

again, are present
in me—the blessing, the rough
passage of the words

that needle silence
needle of history, sharp
family blood drops

7.

the fountain at dusk
swallows its own music—sad
notes in dying light

8.

every created
being needs some forgiveness
the grave won't forgive

it's up to us—there
were things you didn't do right
the mistakes you made

just living is hard
enough, who knows how to keep
a girl's perfect heart

all I know is I
was growing like a woods in
the unformed dark of

your hope, the bad dreams
yet to come, the marriage to
my father who loved

and tormented us
the deaths of your beloved
mother and father

and still I'm growing
toward something though I know
not what, beloved

9.

a night wind walks by
whoosh...dark eyes, an old gray head
enter the forest

Migration

Many birds forming
one bird, a child's
charcoal scrawl made of embers; flickering
afternoons when the eye flares
skyward and imagination cools
to memory—a quick grace-
ful stroke released
above an intemperate horizon.
On a clear day, in a bleak January
of days, this welcome dissolving
arrangement: Something wild
and beautiful passes over,
weaving out of that vast
mapping, a direction hope follows
past vision, to a South
of the mind, a Paradise
of wishes.

III.

Replay

My mother in the garden
balanced

on the brick
edge of the fountain

She doesn't know
the rivers of blood inside her

will soon overflow

that the brain dam will break

the sea levels rise

that hemorrhage will crash
through the gurney's spillways
the banks of the ER

Her skull is still
a whole note

Her ribcage
a musical staff

She's joyous
in this moment, beside the jasmine's
sleeping eyes

with the frost-grass
all around her, the world
wrapped in parchment

Innocent

The moon rose like a dose
of Valium before my father's eyes—

(he swallowed his guilts, buried
his lies, and loaded us up

for a twenty year ride.)
Now he wears the moon

on his lapel—white peony,
white carnation moon—it lights

his face like an innocent
with its gardenia-bright mystery,

wherever—whatever—he is now.
My father the serial liar, serial gambler,

serial loser, with the sweetness
of white moonflower

light in his heart.

Cemetery Song

Who is to say
they aren't tucked into the ground
to sweeten it, like lavender

sachet?
How can we be sure
they aren't sublimely gathered

together
into a deathless bouquet—
swaying in a vessel

of starshine;
ghostly and fresh
in their roomy arrangements?

Tell me I am not
planted here alone, among the silent
stones, chiseled glyphs—

A Visit from the Friendly Aunts

We always intended to reappear
through the night door, the dream floor.
Nothing could keep us away from here.

We knew that death was a veneer
we'd strip away when we got bored.
We always intended to reappear.

Now that we're dust it's easy to steer
our little boats toward your shore.
Nothing could keep us away from here.

We knew how much you missed us, dear;
we blew in from the cosmos like spores.
We always intended to reappear

and here we are, materialized near
your bedroom door, *almost* like we were before.
Nothing could keep us away from here!

(All this ghost stuff is only travel gear.)
We came to buoy you, *esprit de corps.*
We always intended to reappear—
Nothing could keep us away from here.

Angelic Laundromat

Near the intersection at Freeport and Florin,
there's a coin-op where the angels drop in

to wash their week's load of dirty work-wings.
They prop their blue Cheer boxes on the big top

loaders and whirl off, tumbling through the double
glass doors during spin-dry, dressed for sexless

foreplay in their transparent skins. Now you know
this is the impossible country of imagination we are in,

the wide cross-streets of the poem. That is why the angels
wink down at us with such sly grins, as they hang out

the rumpled costumes of the newly dead on a long line
to dry, as they circle the updrafts in see-through grace.

In the Ghost-Time

October stillness sheets all around me.
The last sunlight crawls over my hundreds of minutes.

Twilight in the ghost-time.
Old women head to another life.

Camellias open but they give up nothing.
The valley stars are humble and vanishing.

My grandfather's ukulele strums itself near a silence.
A few lonely notes creep into my pocket.

Turning Sixty

Strangely, it is day.
Beside the upright violin with its
four broken strings, I am feeling lost,
which is a familiar silence.

Everywhere and nowhere, the sunlight.
I am deaf to it all
and I stop here, where I am.
I forget about the blossoms wishing me well
and the summer.

I forget the warm grass with its thousand ways.
The grass giving up its existential scent.
Everywhere.

Old as I feel, young as I was.

I remember yesterday, the hopeful philosopher, the mystic.
I remember a story hidden behind the leaves,
the rich veins of tomorrow in the sky.
The gate

unlocked, opening into forget-me-nots.
I remember laughter,
a boy-ghost's lost frown.

This wasn't what I wanted to write
hovering all day inside my cave
without my inner music.

Poppies At Sunset

The day seethes salts under the quiet
yards. Bone fingers, crisp, dry mouths.

Against a fence, an exhausted paradise
of spoiled petals, a lost poppy tropics.

Hot neon shavings, wind-whittled.
(Without petals they're more exotic—

swollen, blush-pink peduncles
in an anti-world etched by Bosch.)

Billows of three-toed poppy leaves trouble
a slug intent on inching past, to his homely shadow-

hedge, his root-hinged house. Finicky and frail
a doddering recluse hobbles toward a rosy

undertuft of seed swell. *Oh but night is*
slipping quickly

along the feathery edges! Lights out
soon for us too.

Walking Home From the Sacramento Jazz Festival

Old Sacramento, 2004

Thickets of rosemary shrouded in spider
webs above the curb, as if we'd disturbed
something ancient, the air in a sealed

room, a king's burial vault, a pharaoh's
tomb, though the sun and the delta breezes
dispel any actual gloom. I imagine

a Matisse putting up his easel, shaking
out his brushes, setting out his paints,
or an Atget with his heavy camera, or

a Weston with his tripod and lens trained
on the webbing's minutiae so the cross-
weavings appear to be glacial trappings

of the Miocene, mountains draped in ice,
as we walk by with the sounds of jazz
floating in the distance behind us,

gold bass notes, saxophone and banjo
driftings, wafting our way. I think of
a Louis Aggasiz crouched beside the green

tangle, the pointillist blue flowers—magnifying
glass in hand, sun burning through
its disc, enlarging a drosophila's husk,

a piece torn from a skipper moth's
wing, lighting up some idea in the mind
of error and magnificence.

Rainy Picnic at Cosumnes River Preserve

1.

Our picnic is anything but plain: grilled asparagus
with shitake mushrooms, cherries, rosemary

potato chips, local wine—and water of course, to wash things
down. I think of how, in Sanskrit legend, Vamanadeva poked

a hole in the material universe, to let the pure water of Causal
Ocean pour through as the Ganges River—

but this is the San Joaquin—the 21st century—no place here
for holiness to stream forth from its glacial cave.

2.

Someone swears to hear the *plunk plunk plunk*
of raindrops on a pond's clouded eye.

3.

An oak's canopy isn't enough—downpour swarms
through, driving us into a nearby barn.

We tour the place: On a weathered plank above
a weathered beam, Father Hopkins' pied beauty—

cup of dry gleanings—sedges, needlegrass, cropped
tules—a swallow's nest spackled with droppings,

marbled excrement; unlikely stucco
with four furzy golf ball crowns (four chicks,

downy as newborn humans)

4.

—then: carnage
on the barn floor—an abandoned nook

in the rafters: cracked bones, regurgitated
feathers, wings strewn like skeletal leaves—

the local Owl God
with its heart-shaped face, voracious.

Outside in the distance and mist,
a white-tailed kite flies up from a dying

live oak; lifts... *falls*... lifts... *falls*
back—gaunt hawk tethered to the wrist

of its falconer—as if some deathless
spirit was trying to rise,

5.

but the tree held it prisoner.

The Moon Is Doing the Australian Crawl

but down here the thoughts are
subaqueous

the branches of sycamores and elms float up
like kelp or eel grass and sea stars shine

in the memory currents
my mother has worked her way up

through the wave-rungs
of the spirit-corps' fleshless ladder—

secretary of the afterworld
she reentered as grit

                    from the slopes
my brother sifted her in

inched his way down the steeps at Kaneohe
                    to disperse her

close as he could get
to surf-swell, to give her wind

and sea wings

for Rick

Graveyard Shift

Harter's Peach Cannery, 1967

1.

Fluorescent and stainless
we began sorting at dusk,

arms sleeved in slush—slick,

sticky sweet;
the moon became the stone
of a vague fruit unpeeling

the dense valley nights.

2.

We told ourselves it wasn't so
bad, those nights

of burning peach, those rivers
of peach

that drenched our arms
in itch, in spoor of fruit

fly. When the sun oozed up
on the horizon, we stripped,

washed,
and headed home.

3.

Some had lived this way
—it seemed
like forever—my friend Linda's mother,
for twenty-five years—

capped and gowned
in bandage-white, nurse
to the tedious.

4.

Years later
I think of all those hands,

the tiredness of wrists;
how they dipped down into the wet
fuzz and peach silt—

how even the rare
white peaches

made our muscles grow
stiff—how sometimes I felt

dizzy, and went limp:
Vertigo of self
above the belts.

5.

There's a peach silt light
in the sky this evening,
an apricot sun
paring itself

down to a dark pit; splashes
of night and river.

Soon the stars will come clear
as pebbles in a cold current;

they will shiver like fruits
in the orchards of being,
sprouting new shoots

among the endless rows.

Do You Ever Have This Feeling

Do you ever have the feeling that
you are standing inside the first atom
of yourself, that you reside
at the very center of yourself
like the stone in a peach?

Tonight you will
try to pass into the body of another, as water
enters the corpus of earth.

Sometimes there's a buzzing inside you
like a nest of sacred bees.

You wake and light shakes out clear
bursts of gold wings over your eyes.

IV.

Pear Blossom and Cherry Blossom

after Mandelstam

Pear blossom and cherry blossom argue with me.
Their wisdom is ephemeral but they convince.

Wheels of good fortune, they coalesce;
Milky Ways among galaxies of branches.

Floret light and human light, our atoms
embrace. Filament wicks fire up; blink

alive like splintered sunlight. Anther-lanterns blast
apart. Some truth inside us changes shape,

roots itself elsewhere. *Every truth has at least*
nine lives, my ananthous bee-soul instructs.

Soliloquy

1.

This morning the steady groan of a leaf blower down the street
may as well be the hell-bent moan of hard summer wind grinding
things down, clearing the dead layers and years of blossoming.

They tried to force her smile and dressed her in fake
yellow. I had watched the smile unravel; it took ten years.
(What man has torn asunder let no mortician put together.)

Even among those who practice for death, those who rehearse
over and over, who among those will be ready when the last
leftover star tears itself loose from under a cooled eyelid?

2.

Deborah says depression but I don't believe it, the trees don't either,
nor do the flowers I bought at Farmer's Market yesterday: butterfly
bush, lavender, sweet William, wild goldfields, seafoam statice.

Some mornings are still crammed with green light and existential
fervor: filling the pond, feeling the trickle of water from the hose,
knowing the tomatoes are fattening, the tart nasturtiums thriving.

There is a Matisse inside us, bedridden, doomed but snipping the mind's
theater, putting it all together, surrounded by a sea of scalloped leaves,
loves made of colored paper, the exact bright shade we wanted.

3.

My friend sends me a magic toad for good cheer, good luck; the kabuki
Gama rises like storm behind a samurai's head. Its lips are sealed, its eyes
glitter like sky-flash. (In the old days, would we have swallowed the opium?)

The shoji screen that filters the light with its washi paper sheen
makes me feel I'm breathing inside some ancient temple, say Phoenix
Hall in Byodo-in. Outside, the day moon's toothless grin.

4.

I continue to study the primitive and enlightened architecture of the trees—
dogwood today—the berries as they suck the light with their puckered nipples.
I need a new lexicon. My *Descriptionary* is no help. Start here, my pencil advises.

Viburnum

Tonight I write by the light of *viburnum*,
its shining raiment, radiant umbels—
the way Emerson wrote on shipboard

by sea fire, in the middle of his prodigious
terror of the graveyard sea.
I cut the clusters early last evening

while the ghost moon's birch bark
floated overhead and the quiet river
of neighborhood life streamed on

around me. You were not
here to see how I tied the stems
together with a yellow string

so they billowed from a sturdy center
when I set them into water in a blue
and white bowl. They hummed

in silence against the silence,
making this music that entered
and would not leave. So tonight,

as you travel a strange city's
star routes to your sister's bedside,
I plant myself solidly here, in the vast

wave of unquiet your absence
wakes, and think of the corporeal body,
how the mystery of viburnum insists on

singing in mine, reflecting and holding
some luminous presence that lives
inside this otherwise empty hour.

Pink Crape Myrtle

You can approach it
from every angle—the blossoming
tree, the showy burst

of pink-laced, see-through
sky-dapple, the web of slender
branches, ruffled tips.

You can listen for the *shushing*
sound the branches make

as wind rushes through, fresh
from the sloughs, the mud
and silver ditches, fingers of river;
or you can hear

the ocean's breath in it,
or a soul's fluid pouring forth
from the body like sacred oil.

You can curl under its sheen
in an afternoon hour, tune
in to the furious *a capriccio*

singing (as if for its very life!)
a house finch commences
among the crinkled panicles—
or you might

focus instead on the bare
winter tree, a prison of branches,
the way the stripped limbs

will float on far
into spring, insistent, refusing to break
into blossom with the rest

—so late, so almost
out of place among the frilled trumpets,
juicy cups, gaudy perfumes.

Map of the Atmosphere

If you see a shadow
it's no shadow—it's me.
—Eugenio Montale

1.

Already it's mostly over: the ruler
laid down, the line drawn, the years penciled in
inches. One yellow smear

of highlighter for where I am right now, a dot
in space. *Where am I now?* (In a half-lit corner, reading
about the death of a poet, his last conversation

with someone severe, someone in a black hat...)
Outside, a red paper lantern
wobbles in the wind.

2.

It's raining so hard inside the shed
of my heart I sometimes think the flood-
waters must rise, the creeks

overflow, my diligent spirit-boat
sink to the bottom of its lifelong wish
for buoyant days when thoughts open

into melodious blooms, into praise-poems. Yes,
its pouring down while I stare inside through grief's
wide eyes at a sadness, at how difficult

an afternoon can be, even in the middle
of spring, even with the dogwoods' blossoms
lighting the inner dark.

3.

I can see how the old voices might say spirit
in the leaves, as the wind catapults them
toward me—sycamore and linden, gingko

and ash; coppers, carnelians, amber jewels—
so alive in the dying!—each of us preparing
for deluge, what the TV meteorologists are calling

an "atmospheric river" headed our way.
(The magnolias are unbelievers, all green
gloss; impervious, unmoved.) A sycamore leaf

floats down before me, landing on wet asphalt
like an ancient tablet, the veins dried-up
scripts. An entire familiar world is erasing

itself before my eyes. I'm walking through
a soon-to-be tabula rasa, a vanishing
bible of leaves.

4.

The ants march in columns like good
little Nazis, carting the bodies of the dead
to some place hidden, a camp

for the poisoned or those with bitten-off heads.
They scale the walls of an iceberg
rose, and surround the glowing glassworks

at the center of the floating city. Imagine
pollen-lit factories, workers blowing molten gobs
into honey wicks, fragrant goblets; imagine

each rose standing in for every sweet
and impossibly fragile thing, as soldiers begin
to pillage the city in broad daylight.

5.

A third self popped out of my body: *I'm leaving
you*, it said—smiling down from above
with a bicuspid gleam.

The place on my forehead where
it had pried itself loose puckered up
like a pink anthill.

Medusa

The rubbery apple
blossom, sea-tinted body still
perfectly intact; the colors clear
as the annealed century-
old glass flowers in temperature
controlled cases at Harvard.

Looking less real—a plastic
soap bubble blown through
a bright salt hoop of ocean.

Millenniums of useful tricks
in the universe's random book
on order had propelled it
only here: The poisonous
gone astray again.

Tentacles like beaded curtains,
matted among papery grasses, barnacle
encrusted seaweed pompoms.

Afraid of its sting, I poked it
with a driftwood stick. I pried at it
like cruelty, then left it
to the gull's beaks.

Listen,
some mystic might call it
the shining knuckle of Yahweh's
fist, the one that thrust
Lucifer from Heaven.

Poem for the Pandemic: A Secular Prayer

1.
Today a dogwood stood before me
like a towering god dressed in pink
and something inside me bowed to it,

something inside me chanted a hymn,
a prayer, a blessing for dogwoods
in the middle of spring, in the middle

of the pandemic blowing this human
world apart, chewing it up into tiny bits,
minuscule viral drops and drips.

The bees were humming inside
like a choir, like monks at matins or lauds
—zipping and zooming and hovering

among the splay of petals and branches
(unaware they too are vanishing).

2.
The sky is a ruined cathedral
but the crows still worship there;

the finches gather together like poets
about to give a benefit reading,

about to turn breath into song,
about to join hands in secular prayer,

hoping their voices might salve
the saved, while the sun listens in

wearing its mask of smoke—
while two counties away

the trees have become candles,
votives turning to ash.

3.
We flow through the days and the days
flow into us. The cold flows into us—pungent
leaf smells and wood smoke. Autumn
flows into us, equinox and the light's retreat.
Crackling sounds of boots on an icy sidewalk.

All day our death flows into us. That survivor
the November moon cannot stop it. Beethoven
flows into us, with Dvorak, and Bach.
Crow flows into us; he drifts inside lazily,
like an I-Ching hexagram; our death

glides invisibly beside him.

4.
Chalk drawings on the sidewalk.
Spirit-shapes.
Rain-washed cave paintings

that once lived crowded inside
the dark scrawl within
a child's tousled head—

faded pastel pictograms.
The trees feign worship
with an altar of leaves.

Hummingbird Hawkmoth

(Macroglossum stellatarum)

Clear-eyed, I shake the night's
dusts from my wings, the shadow-
strings, the death webs

and dart
like the ruby-throated
hummingbird they've named

me after, and plunge
like hawk into the deep-
funneled throats

of flowers—fuchsias, trumpets,
the yellow ruffles of squash
blossoms—

my quick tongue
an instrument for the nectars
of day, a highway

for its vegetal sugars. (They say
I can nip a hundred flowers
in five minutes

and they're not wrong.)
If I had the beak
or the talons of a god

I would seize the mouse
of temporality instead
and crack its bones.

Votive

The rice fields had dried to stubble, stalks;
I bowed my head and spoke to a flock
of egrets scattered in the glare there.
Then something in the sun's bright eye broke

and a string of clouds passed over where
the egrets' wings shifted and stirred.
I bowed, yes—but not in prayer.
I felt a flame rise, layer by layer.

The tinder-scene before me blurred
until all I saw were these two words:
Lord Egret. (I feel a thirst even now
for that symbolic bird.) Spurred

by that thought I made a silent vow
to write it all down, to detail how
time had slowed to some tick-tick
of eternity's whir.

O'Keeffe's *Jack-in-the-Pulpit II*

This jack shouts through a swollen microphone.
Its hitchhiking spadix nabs us with a bruised thumb—

("in the pulpit" means the minister's collar
is a flare of undone. It shifted gears somewhere

in the before-universe of blank artist's mind, and blared
forth like a purple fantasy of Father Mozart—the hood

became a windblown noise, a trumpet of hemorrhaged
maroon.) It wears a bandage below the waist,

like any stunned heavyweight fighting past prime.
—Bloody thumb. Passion trips us.

The jack hot-wires that message home—
though the jolt is offset with lambent greens—

with a thousand jittery bells of life-force
blasting from all its bright seams.

Economies of Being

I could not bear
to throw it out, the leftover
salad—too pretty, and the leaves
took so long to arrive;

each one like a landscape
seen from above,
with a river and tributaries—

dark green against the oranges
in a bowl the exact
color of larkspur.

So I ate it
with oil and vinegar,
with sprinkles
of pepper and salt.

I chewed each bite
slowly, like someone who has gone
a long time without food,
though I felt no

bodily hunger.

Fireweed

(Epilobium augustifolium)
"the species comes rapidly into burned and destroyed areas..."
—California Mountain Wildflowers

Like avalanche lilies, they heal
earth's blistered skin:
A careless match, lightning
in high blue spruce ignites
spikey racemes along fire-
swept slopes—airborne,
the fuzzy pods undress, descend,
shower downy, tufted puffs.
For once good news travels swiftly.

We travel in wide circles,
skirting the pinkish
brush, where infant stalks
push up. We
venture inward but
step lightly, not wanting
to crush the lovely.
It will take years
for the pines to turn
green, for amber
rings to form precisely
inner eyes. Now the masked
raccoon sleeps the burned-
out hollows. Sunlight seeps through

its gutted crib. Glowing
Chernobyl pollinates the sky,

sinks, slowly, into molten
fields. If all goes well
this forest will reclaim
its piney steeples, scenting the dark
bark of the mountain
chickadee's hutch.

The scarred black trunks rise
around us—crumbled
stumps, ashen roots let go
their tenuous grips; limbs rip, branches crack.
But the birds have returned, dusky
grouse and nuthatch, along with the small
creeping things that were not burned.

Close pink buds droop
open, split into mouths or bells or tiny
alarms; splayed pink tongues
spit sticky cream-colored stars—
whole galaxies loft and float,
sway and dangle—jittery crab-like stigmas.
Spools of ice unwind into clouds
above us, our pale city
limbs out of place, touching
spider-white stamens
where sweet, yellow pollen silts
the wingtips of bees.

We are stung by
the simple wisdom
of visible things. Fireweed
burns away some stubborn

membrane behind our eyes.
We turn back to the car.
We kiss. We turn again

our resilient bodies to the wind.

Gatherer's Alphabet

Archive day, night, spring, summer, autumn, winter—be an apothecary of wonder. Arrange an arsenal of antidotes called art. Admire avocets and arachnids.

Bottle up buddies, beauty, and even brambles. Bravos to Buddha, to butterflies and to brash buddleia bouquets.

Collect coriander, carpenter bees, carnivals and carp. Consort with the condemned.

Dive into the country of Being. Dive in unafraid.

Elope with crow on the coldest morning of your life.

Fish with the ghosts of salmon; drag the river for their sister's bones.

Get greedy. Get down on your knees. Greet the grass with a kiss.

Haul hope in, big truckloads of it. Build big hills of it in your backyard. Hoard it along with any hugs.

Invent a tool for digging up one fat root to anchor you.

June is the time to gather jars of jasmine and jewelweed.

Keep your kitchen stocked with keepsakes: kestrels, Kyries, kisses and kites.

Lip the shine from snail trails, trout scales. Add "lusty" to your lexicon. Listen. Lap gold from Limoges.

Make a gatherer's list. Make a map then abandon it. You are only a mist.

Notebooks are good for the illusion of containing. N is for "nihilist equals nil."

Oleanders, orchestras, orchids and Omar Khayyam, under the O's.

Pack your parlor with plethora—parakeets, poetry and plum jam.

Quietly become the queen of quantum.

Roundup the red diamonds of sunset, the repertory of river reeds.

Sorrow has its own saloons, filled with soldiers and suicides.

Tease the shadows out of hiding. Tally the dead but also the truth of the living.

Utter the name of each thing at least once. Understand the word as umbilicus.

Verbs, vines, veins, verisimilitude and venom should appear in your variorum.

Whole-souled, wholeheartedly grab the world. Whoop it up. Weep.

X out the Xeroxed inkblot you think stains your soul.

Yoke yourself to yellow, to the life-giving yarrow. Yearn. Yawp. Yowl.

Zoom the zones of the ineffable—life zips by. Leave your mark like... *Zorro!*

Self-Portrait as a Green Heron

There is a Gregorian chant
in my left ear; when I take my morning
walk it drowns out all the sorrows.

Deaf in one ear, blind
in one eye—that's the curse
I've always feared.

(My father's spirit was deaf—
he couldn't hear what our hearts were
singing over our morning tea.)

When I am alone I play
the harmonica; no one to elude
except myself.

I am like the green
heron, a timid bird in secluded
ponds, seeking cover.

Narcissus

In January, many gray voices wheedle
Time to give up...

The leaves left on the shivering
limbs seem to listen.

The wind makes them tremble
like toothless old men,

to teach us a lesson.

But the paper whites, fresh from sleep,
aroused, want us to love them

more than our despair.
We believe them

when they promise us the stars,
when they whisper sweet

nothings in our ear.

August Morning

Waking this morning to what felt like a rumbling
sound in the earth, the scent of lavender
from your pillow caught on a breeze.

The world seemed fragile and strange—
which of course, it is—

the rumbling sound was the rescue squad
three houses down. It's too early yet
to tell if someone died—

the elderly woman we see only rarely
(shuffling up the path to the house
with her walker)

or the balding man who guides her
—her son.

The basset and terrier next door are howling,
the fragrances from the rose garden there
are wafting in through the open window

and morning glories twine the fence outside.
I tidy the bed, smooth your pillowcase
and breathe in once again

its lavender aroma.

Tuberose

And how can that beauty
ever die?

Even if it vanishes
something utterly real
will burn day

and night, an indelible
fragrance, a potent cloud
of memory-perfume.

Out of every
death some wand
of the everlasting is
borne up.

A single stalk
rises, a fat match-tip
of cream

which the servants who travel
in secret, cloaked in the heat of late
summer sun will strike
into luminous light.

Autumnal Equinox

The stars clicked on
late; I lounged aimlessly
in my room. Outside,

crazed moths were sucking
and grazing the crimped lips
of trumpet flowers.

It seemed like
everyone I knew had something
precious to give away

—some mystery
free for the taking.
When I lifted my face

from a book, I remembered
every happiness, every
kindness ever

accorded me.

Acknowledgements

Many thanks to the journals where the following poems first appeared, sometimes in earlier versions:

Calliope: "Watercolor"

Cha: An Asian Literary Journal: "Two Geishas on an Anonymous Print, 1923"

Cimarron Review: "Fireweed"

Clade Song: "I Ordered a Dragonfly", "Self-Portrait as a Green Heron"

Clockwatch Review: "Angel with Cabbage Leaf Wings"

Coal Hill Review: "Sewing Box"

Comstock Review: "Gatherer's Alphabet"

Crosswinds: "August Morning"

Cutbank: "Toward the Music"

Ekphrasis: "*The Sea, Cape Split*"

Hawaii Review: "In the Ghost-Time", "Migration"

International Literary Quarterly: "O'Keeffe's *Jack-in-the-Pulpit*"

KXPR Monthly Magazine: "Maggie's Garden"

Levure Litteraire: "Do You Ever Have This Feeling"(reprint), "The Thorne Miniatures: English Bedchamber"

Mockingbird: "Medusa"

Mudlark: "Soliloquy", "Cemetery Song", "Poem for the Pandemic: A Secular Prayer", "Votive", "Economies of Being", "Hummingbird Hawkmoth"

Munyori: "The Reliquary of St. Therese of Lisieux", "Sonnet"

North American Review: "My Mother at Evening", "A Visit from the Friendly Aunts"

One Dog Press: "Maybe I Have No Ideas"

Poecology: "Magpiety"

PoetryMagazine.com: "Love's Animal"

Poetry Northwest: "Lily Sutra"

Prairie Schooner: "Narcissus", "Angelic Laundromat"

Redactions: "Turning Sixty"

Red Wheelbarrow: "Brother Mockingbird"

Spillway: "The Kiss"

Spoon River Poetry Review: "Snow Queen"
String Poet: "After My Mother's Death/Forget-Me-Nots", "Pink Crepe Myrtle"
Suisun Valley Review: "Callas"
The Moth: "Wedding Guest"
The Normal School: "Map of the Atmosphere"
The Wayfarer: "Pear Blossom and Cherry Blossom"
Tule Review: "Do You Ever Have This Feeling"
Vox Populi: "Angel Behind Bars", "The Moon Is Doing the Australian Crawl", "Autumnal Equinox", "Maybe I Have No Ideas" (reprint)
Weber: The Contemporary West: "Morro Bay Sketch", "How the River Sleeps", "Poppies at Sunset", "Tuberose", "Static", "Jeffers at the Edward Weston Show", "Critic"

Thanks also to the editors of the anthologies below for including these poems:
Claiming the Spirit Within (Beacon Press): "Toward the Music"
The Doll Collection (Terrapin Books): "Cloth Doll with Found Feathers"
I've Always Meant to Tell You: Letters to our Mothers (Pocket Books): "To My Mother on her Seventy-Sixth Birthday"
Know Me Here (WordTemple Press): "Callas"
Morning Thunder Poems (Plumas County Arts Commission): "Calling the Horses"
Sacramento Voices (Cold River Press): "O'Keeffe's Jack-in-the-Pulpit", "Snow Queen", "Rainy Picnic at Cosumnes River Preserve", "Graveyard Shift", "Walking Home from the Sacramento Jazz Festival", "How the River Sleeps"
What The Redwoods Know (WordTemple Press): "Walking Home from the Sacramento Jazz Festival"

A number of the poems here also appeared previously in the print chapbooks *Feather's Hand* (Swan Scythe Press, 2000), *To a Small Moth* (Poet's Corner Press, 2002), *Susan Kelly-DeWitt Greatest Hits 1983-2002* (Pudding House Publication, 2003), *The Book of Insects* (Spruce Street Press, 2003), and *The Land* (Rattlesnake Press, 2005).

"Viburnum" was an Honorable Mention in the Tor House Poetry Prize, 2003.

Author's Note

First of all, many thanks to David Starkey and Chryss Yost of Gunpowder Press, for making this collection happen—it has been an honor and a privilege to work with them.

I also want to express my ongoing gratitude to the poets and dear friends whose support, advice, encouragement, and friendship have sustained me, especially Sandra McPherson, Joshua McKinney, Bob Stanley, Joyce Jenkins, Mary Mackey, Ilya Kaminsky, Russell Thorburn, Hannah Stein, William Slaughter, Shawn Pittard, Maya Khosla, Michael Simms, and my poetry pals, Mary Zeppa, Kathleen Lynch, Lisa Abraham Dominguez, Victoria Dalkey, Catherine French and our dear Carol Frith (who passed away in 2020), and to my beloved mentor Dennis Schmitz, who passed away in 2019.

Big thanks also to Sandra McPherson, Michael Simms, Maya Khosla and Lee Herrick for their good words on this book's cover! And, finally, biggest thanks to my partner in life, David DeWitt, for his almost five-times-ten years of affection and support—and to my children, Jennifer and Michael, and my son-in-law Michael Shen for being the delightful and creative people they are.

About the Poet

Sacramento resident Susan Kelly-DeWitt is the inaugural poet in the California Poets Series. She is a former Wallace Stegner Fellow and the author of *Gravitational Tug* (Main Street Rag Publishing, 2020), *Spider Season* (Cold River Press, 2016), *The Fortunate Islands* (Marick Press, 2008), and a number of previous small press and online collections. Her work has also appeared in many anthologies, and in print and online journals at home and abroad. Her past professional and writing life includes having been a reviewer for *Library Journal*, the editor-in-chief of the online journal *Perihelion*, the Program Director of the Sacramento Poetry Center and the Women's Wisdom Arts Program, a Poet in the Schools and a Poet in the Prisons, a blogger for *Coal Hill Review*, and a longtime instructor for the UC Davis Division of Continuing Education. She is currently a member of the National Book Critics Circle, the Northern California Book Reviewers Association and a contributing editor for *Poetry Flash*. She is also an exhibiting visual artist. For more information, please visit her website at www.susankelly-dewitt.com.

BARRY SPACKS POETRY PRIZE SERIES

2015
Instead of Sadness
Catherine Abbey Hodges

2016
Burning Down Disneyland
Kurt Olsson

2017
Posthumous Noon
Aaron Baker

2018
The Ghosts of Lost Animals
Michelle Bonczek Evory

2019
Drinking with O'Hara
Glenn Freeman

2020
Curriculum
Meghan Dunn

2021
Like All Light
Todd Copeland

Also from Gunpowder Press

The Tarnation of Faust: Poems by David Case

Mouth & Fruit: Poems by Chryss Yost

Shaping Water: Poems by Barry Spacks

Original Face: Poems by Jim Peterson

What Breathes Us: Santa Barbara Poets Laureate, 2005-2015
Edited by David Starkey

Unfinished City: Poems by Nan Cohen

Raft of Days: Poems by Catherine Abbey Hodges

Mother Lode: Poems by Peg Quinn

and the Shoreline Voices Projects:

Buzz: Poets Respond to SWARM
Edited by Nancy Gifford and Chryss Yost

Rare Feathers: Poems on Birds & Art
Edited by Nancy Gifford, Chryss Yost, and George Yatchisin

To Give Life a Shape: Poems Inspired by the Santa Barbara Museum of Art
Edited by David Starkey and Chryss Yost

While You Wait: A Collection by Santa Barbara County Poets
Edited by Laure-Anne Bosselaar

Big Enough for Words: Poems and Vintage Photographs from California's Central Coast
Edited by David Starkey, George Yatchisin, and Chryss Yost

CPSIA information can be obtained
at www.ICGtesting.com
Printed in the USA
JSHW042340161122
33322JS00001B/40

9 781957 062006